THE WALL MENDERS
by Kate Noakes

Kate Noakes lives in Caversham, and is studying for an MPhil in Creative Writing at the University of Glamorgan. She has lived in California and South Australia. This is her second collection of poetry.

By the same author:
Ocean to Interior (Mighty Erudite 2007)

First published in the UK in 2009 by

Two Rivers Press
35–39 London Street
Reading RG1 4PS
www.tworiverspress.com

Two Rivers Press is represented in the UK by Inpress Ltd. and distributed by Central Books

Cover design: Pip Hall
Photo: Frances Sutton
Printed and bound in Great Britain by
CPI Antony Rowe, Chippenham and Eastbourne

ISBN 978-1-901677-64-5

Acknowledgements

I am very grateful to Gillian Clarke for her insightful
and rigorous readings of the drafts of these poems,
as well as to Sheenagh Pugh, Christopher Meredith,
Tony Curtis and Philip Gross for their suggestions
and corrections.

Earlier versions of some of these poems appeared
in the following: *Revival, South* and *Square.*
'The wall menders' was the runner up in Leaf Books
spring 2008 poetry competition and 'The meaning
of dormant' won the 2008 Rhyme and Reason
poetry competition.

Dedication

And suddenly the noise

of my life is gone, the house falls
back to immersion hum, a tap
left to run and the buzz of my ears, thinking.

You are out to walk or bike, disturb skylarks,
wonder at kites. I am here, busy
under a quilt of paper and books.

Contents

PART II | MORTAR AND LIME

Part I – Taking a hammer

Suffolk beach

The east unsettles in its flatness,
far horizons, father of all skies,

the way the land surrenders
to the sea with a sigh,

a sliding-under of shingle,
how marsh and fen seem

to sink, shift underfoot,
bedrock's unstable coverlet.

I've slept on discomfort, this pea
under a mattress has kept me awake.

The sun on the sea should be
always setting, water swallowing fire,

not this disconsoling birth of light,
barely warming the dead.

Choosing our grave goods

Something half-precious is hiding
in mould and damp leaves,

chosen from a lifetime's treasure -
a fractured geode, flaky,

tied with twine, each twin half
my cave of crystal and light.

*

Silk perished now by the workings
of worms, tooth metal loosened,

right arm titanium plate with screws,
left hand holding a bicycle chain,

fourth finger gold and platinum ring,
the story of a loved man.

*

A willow stretches high,
its roots nourished by a basket

of blonde hair and long bones
and beside it another

from the same source, busy
taking stream water to the sky.

Call me Kali

If they see a harpy, so let it be.
Change my suit into feathers,
stilettos into talons.

If they hear the voice
of a shrew, so bridle,
scold, parade me.

If they fear blackness
and me, devouring mother,
so blood my tongue.

I'll make a garland
from the heads of my victims,
all one hundred and eight of them.

Imagine my garden

My mind is the place where
no-one can touch me.
I travel to where there's no
somnolent tap, only warm water.

As I lie back on springy moss,
there is no rope burning my skin
just the sun's heat on my nakedness.

My distant home has no
whips, manacles, electrodes,
but the gentle brush of flowers
as I move through the undergrowth.

The trick of condensation

I long for forgotten clouds,
sing for a cloud to float free
from the high winds and drench me,
soak my skin, cold, cold,

to pass on its sleights of hand,
the trick of condensation,
those charges of lightning
and the see-saw,

frost-thaw of hail.
Remember hail?
Ice sweets on the lawn,
sleet, snow even.

April

A white room opens.
Dawn and snow
flakes steady on our walled-in corner.

April throws her weight around,
beats down lime from the beech,
smothers all other greens,

takes control. She lays it heavy
on the land we tend, as fear
turns down our smiles.

Shocked wrens make for cover.
We chase away worries
in an epic fight, our squeals echo.

I record these moments with flash
and pen for Christmas cards,
so it won't be over, can come again.

Dial up, dial up and listen to the melt
sliding from sycamore and pine.
Bamboo springs back like a vaulting pole.

Ruffle-feathered, the wrens clear
their nest. A bi-plane drones.
Sunday playtime.

In the colour supplement an ice-shelf
reflected in the ocean, blue on blue
under a blue sky.

By noon, green is coming through,
the pond is black, but the frog-spawn
is frozen, each comma stopped.

Glacier

Summer, and the ice shrinks faster than ever,
meltwater's filled with crystals in its hurry to be free.

We tell the children not to whinge on the switch-
backed ascent, that they must see the glacier,

feel its gritty surface, touch until their finger-tips
are stuck, iced-in. For their grandchildren they need

to stare into the blue heart, and listen.

The stability of scree

For so many Northern days we have lain
together on the mountain's flank, our limbs
stacked and locked at just the right angles;
thirty degrees of repose for bone and scrawn.

We breathed soft under the massif's roar.
Sprung moss welcomed us into the earth,
lichen brought us cups of orange and gold,
made us part of the warm core.

Sleeping, there is harmony in our stones,
but a restless night, one not greened
by the aurora perhaps, triggers a rock fall
like a fell runner misreading the stability

of scree and we must start over, meshing
our bodies for comfort against the slope.

The fire walk

I began early, barefoot or sandaled,
my child feet grew hard skin,
felt little on beach gravel
or hot tarmac.

On that tropical night, I waited
for copra and charcoal to burn white.
Raked into a lava flow, it made
a path for my true self.

I was too quick for blisters
and made only steam.

My footprints in the embers hardened
into memory, pressed in the clinker
like Eve's in the bedrock
of an African lagoon.

My first Banksy

I tramp along noting spilled chips
and take-away cartons sinking
in the dirt under the railway bridge.

I see a small piece, not
to be mistaken for graffiti,
black stencil on cream car park wall,

a man in a stove-pipe hat,
suited, brief-cased, held aloft
by an open umbrella,

being rescued from work. Diverting,
brings a smile in the gloom.
All that goes down must come up.

Identity

The time came when prints of eye and finger
were required. All were tattooed with silicon,
became readable like dogs and packets of food.

I was logged. The stateless went
back-street to surgeons with fake chips,
skilled at opening and closing key-holes.

One day when I woke and looked hard
in the mirror, I saw familiar faces,
teacher, post-mistress, landlady

and the viper slumbering
in my breast stirred, sparked.

In grimy towns

That succubus love can happen in the time
it takes a bluebottle to lay her eggs
in the still-fleshy head of a Hereford.

While bride-maggots wriggle and gorge
on its cheeks and eyes, a cycle of recrimination
can begin, end and start again.

And as the next generation swarms
on the clean-picked skull
that gave it birth, love moves on,

finds others to fry in the blue hoof marks
of butchers' shop walls in grimy towns
circled by motorways.

Along the Indus

You are lost in a time of drought
where the truth is. rivers no longer
make their way to the sea,

but you don't believe it until
you spend an evening watching.

Fish eagles, talons full, grab at
a feast of plump carp thrashing
in mud pools, and when the heron

move in with their rapier bills,
there's no standing, no ceremony,
just an easy kill.

The bird-headed fishermen
hang up their decoys and gut
the last of their catch, split it

to dry on poles like prayers,
like their skeleton nets.

Clean burn

Here is treacle again, the smell
of brimstone from cottage chimneys
and the insistence of water
down along seams.

This time it's all above ground,
open. Cast your eyes wide
and take in the vast pit,
a black gape
at the head of the valley.

They're shouting in the choke
against collections of dust
and memories of tin bath
and black smoke.

And carrion coal shines, blinds us
with its strip-tease promises
of a clean burn.

The wedding carpet

Today I risked my sitting room of dust,
broke two nails and cut my palms
on a lump of concrete.

I unearthed my wedding carpet, beat it,
shook it with the force of a bomb
and its jewels reappeared.

My children sing now in a patterned tent.
We have no water, food, faith,
but we do have comfort in silk and wool.

Space junk

Earth is like Saturn from far out,
but ringed with precious metal. For all

the precision in its machining, cut
with diamond and laser, this titanium,

platinum, gold, these alloys of nickel
and steel, once stainless, are now

scrap, trimmings on a factory floor,
yet a seam of mineral wealth

circling beyond our reach.
Dangerous debris falls back;

some nights the sky is lit up
by man-made meteors. They may be

new veins to mine if we can find
a way with this orrery of junk.

Foot and mouth journey

Cumbria
In the pre-dawn dark we beach
in the grey. Twisting across rough granite
pine roots fight for footholds.

Where one curls its toes, we tie up
one last time for who knows
how long, forever?

Even wild cats can't drag us
from this sunrise, but a curt notice,
by order, threatens a £5,000 fine.

Devon
Buzzard scans from telegraph pole,
stitchwort winks in banks bled dry,
red silt clogs these familiar lanes.

Hush – a piece of cheese bolts
from yellow-hammer hedge.
Listen to the silence without the lambs.

Staffordshire

The power station spews twenty-four hours
of sulphur. The kiln air is cleaner.

Your Nan no longer scrubs brickwork
to head height, but a new pyre burns,

sending acrid smoke black-billowing
over the twice-lost land.

San Francisco

In this new place we're taken aside
before Customs and quizzed
about the mud on our shoes.

City stuff, we say to deaf ears,
miles from any farm.

Mestra's tale
from Ovid's Metamorphoses

Mestra, daughter of Erysichthon, is raped by Neptune
as a teenager and later, when she is being sold in marriage .
by her father, she calls on Neptune to save her. She is given
the gift of shape-shifting which enables her to escape.
As punishment for his felling her sacred oak tree, Ceres
sends one of her oreads (mountain nymphs) to find Famine
to infect Erysichthon. He is made insatiably hungry.
Having sold his every possession and consumed the
proceeds, Erysichthon, sells the only thing he has left,
his daughter, over and over again.

Think of the hottest day of summer, that starts –
bare feet on the dewy grass, then the sun burning
the cliffs as we bucket and spade it down
to the wide sweep of Barafundle Bay.

Feel warm sand, its inch-down coolness,
remember the smugglers' cave hidden
by black rocks. Now pick it all up,
take it backwards.

I'm young, not girl, not woman. There's no
National Trust car park, no coastal path,
just me on the beach, the gulls
out fishing to the fickle strain of the wind.

I'm in search of perfect shells, unbitten,
and stones with holes for threading.
Head down, on my knees, I crab along
the tide-line of weed and frayed rope.

I check the wave-length and pick my way
into the cave, dark with mussels and salt-stink.
A full scallop shell catches my eye, both halves,
the essence of nacre and pearl.

A wave spins me round, the sea is kissing me,
a tongue of water in my throat. He vanishes,
leaving me with a scarf of kelp
and this gold clam in my hand.

*

I can't tell anyone,
cut off, inundated,
invaded by the sea,
part-drowned,

salted like cod,
prised open
an oyster, mussel
pulled off like a limpet,

left washed up, found,
so much flotsam
at low tide, part of me
ebbed away,

forever out there
on the wave-patterned
sea bed of grit
and fish bones.

*

I ran to the place where comfort grows as a lawn
of fern-shaped mosses in the light-spaces of our wood,
wrapped myself in its blanket and slept deep and long.

Dryads stepped from dogwood stems,
where they fluttered in leaf and bract,
to release my hurt, make it coral spot and earth star
dissolve it through porous bands of chalk.

Waking, I saw the nymph of the holm oak
had appeared, folded me in her new leaves,
stitched with the silver of her heart.

*

The split of crashing timber
is as nothing to the screams
of a dying nymph.

Men with chain saws, band saws,
shredders were deafened
by orange cups.

Only I heard her and came
running, but too late save
to watch her ancient oak fall

with all the dignity of an executed queen.
My father rubbed his palms,
pound signs in his eyes.

Wind stopped the work
and Nature sent Oread
to be revenged on his greed.

*

In a land of billabongs, spinifex
and salt-bush, Famine spent her days
picking over the bones of stranded animals
and grubbing for roots.

Across the plain Oread
searched for her, her calls flattened
into the brittle earth by air heavy
and filled with flies.

After weeks of walking, Oread found her
naked in black-boy bushes
sucking on a yam, her teeth
as brown as her nails.

From a distance she conveyed Nature's
request - a curse on him.
Let him beg to burn incense
and sacrifice bulls.

Famine rose without a word,
clapped her hands, laughed
and in a pall of red dust,
flew up as a locust.

*

In his feathered bed my father slept contented,
dreamed of pound notes and dollar bills
stacked in the safe. The faces on each
taking turns to smile at him.

Famine squatted on his chest,
her tough mandibles sucked fullness
from his belly, replaced it with hunger,
that ravenous boar.

He woke starving the next day,
binged on the contents
of store cupboard and fridge,
demanded more.

*

Breathless, shoreline, doubled over,
waves lapping feet, pressure rising,
no more road to go, eyes to sky,
arms wide, a scream
and in a moment of calm,
a prayer – Save me from slavery.

Take back these shells - I held out
the golden clams, dropped them
one by one into the brine.
With the last one I stopped, closed
my palm, knew the answer.
Something had changed in my blood.

*

I remember how it felt on that strand
in the silence after Neptune had gone.
As you might say, weird, scary, certainly
when I heard Rhys roaring through the
sheep fields
setting off collies as he chased me down,
then, odd, as I slipped into another's skin.

Ever wondered what it's like to be
the opposite of yourself, not forever,
just a day? All I know is for me
it was exactly the same, even bearded
like a sea-dog, which saved me from that
old man,
I was still me, same breath, same eyes,
same thought
And I was convincing, no woman here,
just my bronze hook and the gullible fish.

*

After that first sale, my father got the
timing right
or as near as – the bargain to be struck
before the waxing moon turned full.

I'd have to wait a few days of servitude
and nights of growing cross-eyed
sky-light staring. I never knew

how I would be when my back folded
my arms stretched and my legs
contracted, whether I'd be two-toed,

cloven or clawed, coarse-haired, furred
or feathered, antlered, horned,
snouted, beaked or jowled.

Hind was my favourite: being able to hide
in the merest shade and clear
the earth in one ecstatic bound.

Returning was painful from deer form,
any form and I never knew whose spell
I was under: my father's, Neptune's.

*

Each phase of this repeating story
became predictable as I galloped,
leaped, loped, flew my way home
in the dark hours of morning.

With lead feet I'd take
transforming steps
into my father's house
and feel less and less pity.

Among the crumbs and gnawed bones,
husks, empty bottles, the detritus
of an orgy, he was animal
and thinner day by day,

ribs and hips protruding, skin shrunk
over balding skull, fingers like hen feet,
his body a living hell
and I resented him.

I looked up the definition of
anorexia, bulimia? No tell-tale smells
left me confused, a confused nothing
attracting no notice save a grunt

of recognition as he staggered to bed
empty
holding his aching stomach;
nothing to bully-boy but the ticket
to his next hollow feed.

*

Word got out, it always does
from the aggrieved of north
and south and that was us – done.

We needed to leave town fast,
sell up quickly and go. Someone
got a bargain in our house,

furniture, fittings, odds and sods.
So, I was left with this man
who screamed all day for food.

He ate every penny piece, pot and pan.
I wanted shot of him for good.
In the end his body turned

and started eating from within,
feeding on its own organs,
burning and tearing him.

Me? I went back to your father,
who always saw the softness
beneath my skin.

Part II – Mortar and lime

New year

The rain has washed us back to basics,
back to the building blocks
of flint and sand.

In clay hoof-prints,
small ponds of milk-water
cloud the past,

opening foundations
for us to screed this year.

A call for action
in the gravel-throated cry
of a pheasant

and our spadework begins.

The wall menders

I see him now as a man:
my boy and I work together
making music of boulder and grit,
passing stones over this growing wall.

We fill the brief space between us
with small notes, flat, sharp,
coming closer in building a barrier
that forgets the contours of the fells.

I see him now in the air
and never-harming rain, a man spared
the heat of the pit. We make
our own small monuments.

We were here and we thought about
scored coping, lunkies for sheep;
made stiles and badger smoots
and paused for breath on the mossy clefts.

I might hear the gush of water
pumped from galleries and shafts,
whispers of re-hiring. But I'm too old
and spoiled by the open.

My boy lacks the skills of prop, board
and pick, spends his days
in this uplifting labour, his voice
quavering between whistle and hum.

Peat cutting reprise

May day, with a long winter gone the men
work for the one ahead to be fuelled
this year by turf. Our low homes, washing,
cooking will be fired from the bog.

Older voices guide the young in the stamp
of boot on shaft, the ways of iron in sod
and the making of black squares,
carved with the slope of the cut.

Wet slabs of earth are laid out today
in the smallest of suns. In the few years
we have left it alone, the peat has shrunk,
ponds and runnels have formed.

Our land is preserved now by laws
that reach to even these far islands.

Cobbing

Mud-pie feet are smooth
by mid-September.
Pumice dries on the sink.

Such the properties of clay
and water pressed
into walls each fine day,

their curves merging,
into the folds
of West Country hills.

Earth underfoot daubed
by hand is friendly cob,
the vernacular of tilled fields,

our coloured architecture
defined in wicherts
and dabbins.

When dry, the adobe keeps
and releases moisture, heat,
is good for the chest.

Best when wet, malleable
and our bare feet touch
in its straw nest.

Merino

Mid-summer the boys gathered
from southern places with names
like roo and barra.

Mostly I ignored them. They smelled
of daggy sheep and stale beer,
but one year he caught me

when I saw him lift
an anxious, complaining ewe
and cradle her calm in his thighs.

Perhaps it was the flex of his muscles,
tight under bronzed skin or
the stand-out veins on his arms,

or despite roughness and blunt nails,
his gentle three-minute hands,
buzzing clippers

deep into the staple without
a single nick to her skin.
Maybe it was his freckles,

and the peeling on his nose
or the flash of his smile as he wiped
dust and sweat from his forehead.

It might've been all these,
but if only he'd said a word,
I would have followed.

The white garden

Dark now, a chase of shadows
when the moon dips behind clouds
as you trip-toe, tip-toe home
on flagstone paths, past beds
of low box edging squares.

Lit now by white:
torches of lilies and peonies,
fairy-light gypsophila
and glow worms of jasmine
day-bright in the fullness.

Scent of night stocks,
mock-orange guide you
to the book's new page
and your notes that planned
how this would be.

The meaning of dormant

Pick a seed, any seed
for the womb of hard soil
bouldered with ice. Entomb
this tattooed keeper
of crop mythology.

Think of it as a one-way
bet with the future
held in a glass ovary
just in case we need
to coax it into life.

There's more than one
quiet sphere shuffled here.
Two by two they sleep
at the end of these tubes,
suspended in the permafrost,

safe, until with luck
we find an olive branch
and the meaning of dormant
in a flow of meltwater.

Different weather

Footsore and blistered, hands cracked
and bloody from a day of slash and burn,
Adam collapses into a veranda chair.

Here in the sweat that plasters
blond curls to the back of his neck,
he dreams of different weather,

not rain you can set your watch by,
but the softness of summer
in a Wessex lane and of soil that is stable,

bound by generations of work,
not this fluid stuff that slides
so freely from his grasp.

*

In a frozen field half a world away,
Eve, bundled up against a cutting wind
digs for roots, grubs at a winter living.

She pauses, pulls thin wool
over her head and ties the shawl
tight about her neck, warms

her face behind fingerless gloves
and resumes the slice and drag
of mattock through the clay.

It's March and the watery sun weakens
the clouds for a moment. Something
warming is on its way.

How to garden

There's something curious
in knowing how to garden
by the phases of the moon,

how to plant seeds at the moment
when the soil is just so warm,
has most moisture.

So I buy moon charts, look
for times when the sea is tranquil,
plan the year out on the tides,

but one night I mistake the hour
and flounder about in the dark
planting snowdrops.

Stripping the willow

Punt through the lilied channels,
your pontoon waking the morning,

fat splashes from water voles, cries of grebe
and booms of muddled bitterns.

Watch for the camera eye of a heron
checking on your work,

the boat stacked high with cut stems.
It's hard to leave this for the fast road home,

but last year's harvest woven into horses
and new men has something of it

in the creak of bent wicker and the flick
of switches when you let them go.

Before the barrage

It's semi-religious, waxing my board,
the stroke of a supplicant
praying for a wave.

As I ask for the right grip
between fibre glass
and the soles of my feet,

a swell comes to shift sediments
for the last time, a peak
in the grip of the moon.

It breaks in the estuary,
over salt-marsh and mudflat,
rushing to Severnside.

I see myself riding
that cloud of a wave past
lock gates and cathedrals,

water meadows and tow paths,
from point to down on a cumulous set,
no-one blocking my line,

no drop-ins or snakers,
no board-ditchers, on this
final roll of the Bore.

Harbour-side

You can eat them, I tell her disbelieving eyes.
Gross, no way, she says adding
a grand cone to her collection.

Celebrating shellfish years later,
I take her to the clapboard shed
where the whelk-man, with hands

the size of paddles, makes a few twists
and gives her a bag-full, hopper-fresh,
offers fine vinegar and sea salt.

She takes a plump one, allows
the sharp spume to ebb from her tongue
and bites into that sweet melting flesh.

Until she balls the sodden paper and tosses it
among the stacked lobster pots and rolled nets,
I hear only soft moans and lip-smacks.

Watercress

Think of this as
drinking a clear stream
mineraled with chalk,

a soup so clean
the purity of mustard
fills your throat.

Take this bunch
of vivid green,
the essence of pepper

and let it rush
through your body
alive, oh alive.

Foraging

Boots snap and crunch sticks and leaves.
Our eyes are steeled on branch and ground
for mushrooms, penny buns, chanterelles,

beryl cobs of nuts, nettles and hairy bittercress.
We straighten our backs in the sometime silence
between pheasant cry and the wing beat

of dog-chased pigeon and march again through
brambled cover, our baskets full with fruit,
rosehip rubies and sloes like a case of minerals.

Mistletoe

He plans ahead for Christmas future, rekindling
the kisses of his youth from these waxy drupes.

He squashes viscin and pearls onto apple branches,
cramming them into all the nooks where mistletoe

might root, as if he was a sticky-beaked thrush.
In time, when it has grown to the size of a globe,

a skeleton of land and ocean silhouetted against
the pale steel, he climbs to the edge of the sky

and releases it to gravity, spends afternoons reducing
its power still more into sprigs for lintels.

At the Farmers' market, I cross his palm with silver,
in the hope of a cure for my faint breath and broken heart.

First catch your fish

For days of Westerlies he monitors the low heat
and quality of smoke until you bring

that filmed muscle of gun-metal
for racking with herring and oysters.

He adds the right wood-chips for flavour,
oak, sometimes hickory

and at the moment when its skin
is shag-brown, its flesh sheened,

he brings down your tender-nursed
salmon for the ceremony of slicing.

With care and the sharpest of knives, he carves
it into leaves, adds mustard and dill,

packs it reverently for the post, so it reaches
your kitchen with all the incense of the north.

Gongfu

He talked of tea as a mystery,
conjured three delicate cups,
invited me to sip fragrance,

while he rolled a name in his mouth,
pu-erh, pu-erh, prize of Yunnan,
best of the south.

As I drank smoke, he revealed fineness
like wine improving, deciphered age
in brick and cake, caressed another pot.

Courage, he said, is losing
the first steep, allowing the leaves
to breathe before showing their secrets.

If only we could follow the hill tribes,
give wild camellia in tribute,
the price for being left alone.

We could make ripe offerings
to placate Party gods
with amnesties of tea.